NLP Guide:

Tips And Methods To Make Others Listen To You

Table of content

Introduction

Humans are really smart because they can use their minds to do different things because the brain works at a super-sonic speed. You can interpret different things and get a quick solution to your problem with the help of your amazing brain. The main goal of every human life is to become a winner, but to become a winner, you should have potential mind skills. You should know how to complete the job by exploiting your psyche. It can be difficult for you to do practically, but with the help of better communication, hypnosis and NLP, you can easily control your mind. It will be good to learn important techniques, improve your life and develop new habits that can bring drastic changes in your life.

NLP stands for Neuro-linguistic programming and this concept helps you to exploit your complete mental power. It pushes you to the edge of excellence and does things that were difficult to you earlier. The NLP was described by Richard Brandler and John Grinder in 1970. This Richard is a self-help writer and the Grinder is a linguistic expert. They worked on previous concepts laid by the experts of neurology and linguistics. They typically focus on the use of both sides of brains and unite the conscious and subconscious minds. Everyone has an active mind aka conscious that helps you to keep awake, but the unconscious and subconscious mind is dormant.

Initially, this concept was new to people and they were unaware of its value. Nowadays, this concept is growing popular. The NLP helps people to draw existing thinking and teaches different ways to a person to get more out of his/her potential. Every human has a lot of mental potentials and it is difficult to fully tap into the potential. With the use of NLP, you can easily tap into the subconscious mind and think out of the box. This theory helps you to learn how to cut down all wrongs in your life and promote the right things. The NLP can be taken as a framework to help you to improve the ability of your mind.

This book will show how you can use all three parts of your mind and do more in your life. The book is divided into numerous chapters to make your work easy.

Chapter 1 – What is NLP? Important Principles and Benefits of NLP

Neuro-Linguistic Programing aka NLP is a most important methodology designed for your help to make dramatic changes in your life. It is based on a basic idea that your physical senses are able to perceive only a small part of this world. Your views are filtered by your beliefs, experiences, assumptions and values. NLP contains numerous techniques that can help you to change your thinking, learn and communicate. For instance, NLP professional can deal with a variety of issues ranging from spiritual beliefs, removing fears from your life, dealing with inner conflicts and procrastination.

Experts can help you to become an effective communicator, increase your motivation, increase your efficiency in personal and professional life and maintain your behavior. With the help of NLP, the human behavior can be functional with your senses. It is a powerful model of experience along with communication. The Neuro-Linguistic Programing symbolizes the relationship between body, brain and language. You can manage your behavior with the help of this program and set of tools.

Change Model

The Neuro-Linguistic Programming change model involves:

- Find out the current state of the person.

- Identify the goals and outcomes (desired state)

- Add suitable resources that can produce the desired outcome

The patterns and techniques of NLP will help you to recognize and define the current state. It helps you to generate and use appropriate resources to get the advantage of ecological modifications in a system.

Fundamental Principles of Neuro-Linguistic Programming

- The map can be taken as terrain.

- Mind and your life are universal processes.

The Neuro-Linguistic Programming can be taken as a manual for your brain. It is a study on your feelings, activities and thoughts marked by the curiosity and you can get positive results. The NLP practice helps you to understand how people organize their language, thinking, behavior and feelings to produce positive results. Your unique internal map is an important thing that helps you to know how your mind filters and recognize different things absorbed with the help of five senses.

Linguistic

Every individual form his/her mental map with the help of language, sounds, internal images, feelings, smells and taste. It helps you to increase your awareness and activate your mind.

Neuro

Every individual has his/her own mental filtering structure for the processing of millions of bits of data absorbed with the help of the senses. The first mental map consists of images, tangible awareness, interior sensations, smells and tastes to form results of the Neuro filtering process. Once you assign personal meaning to the received information from the outside world.

Programming

Behavioral responses occur as a result of the neurological filtering procedures and the succeeding linguistic maps. NLP explores the relationship between your thoughts, emotions, expressions and patterns of behavior. The programs incorporate family therapy, behavioral psychology, information theory, linguistics, anthropology and various other disciplines.

It helps you to explore the relations between your thoughts and emotions. The NLP practitioner uses these relationships to understand the thoughts and activities of a client. This study makes it easy to explore what is important to change and new important skills to adopt. The modeling is the key features of the Neuro-Linguistic Programming.

The NLP is a powerful tool for the management of change and helps people to transform their thinking and working patterns. It can help you to bring major changes in your personal and professional lives. The Neuro-Linguistic Programming is a powerful skill to use in the management of sales, psychology, management, coaching and other forms of personal developments. It consists of an innovative set of tools and procedures to create change.

This powerful disciple helps you to unlock the structure of excellence and communication. This can be helpful for people to increase the efficiency, communication skills, and productivity.

Techniques of NLP

- Anchoring

- Future pacing

- Swish

- Reframing

- Well-formed outcome

- Ecology

- Parts integration

- Visual/Kinesthetic Dissociation

- Metaphor

- State management

- Sleight of Mouth

Benefits of Neuro-Linguistic Programming

The Neuro-Linguistic Programming is a psychological approach to personal development and enhanced communication skills. There are numerous benefits linked with the Neuro-Linguistic Programming:

Supports Your Weight Loss Plans

The eating habits can make it difficult for you to reduce weight because the eaters can't control their appetite. The modification of psychological behavior will help you to reduce the eating methods and tune your mind to increase exercise. The NLP programs help people to get positive benefits of diet and exercise. It will help you get rid of troublesome behavior that can make it difficult for you to do exercise regularly.

Improve Learning Ability

Sometimes, the learning can be a difficult process for you and this can be discouraging for you. The NLP proves helpful to improve your self-esteem and dyslexia by reducing anxiety and increasing relaxation. It can increase your learning capabilities.

Reduce Anxiety and Enhance Mood

If you are suffering from anxiety, the NLP can be helpful to alleviate the feelings of nervousness. It is a useful tool to enhance your mood and get rid of depression and other feelings.

Get Rid of Bad Habits

If you have any bad habit that is affecting your health, you can get the advantage of NLP. This method is free from any side effects and is a great tool to fight with bad habits. If you want to decrease your appetite for junk food, the NLP can be really helpful.

Chapter 2 – How to manage your mind and upgrade yourself?

NLP is an excellent program and its effects can be different for different people. If you want to get the advantage of this approach, you should eat well, get plenty of sunlight, exercise, and mental activities.

Develop Confidence

The confidence is one important thing that can help you in every part of your life. You can increase your self-confidence with the help of NLP. Once you master your ability to gain confidence, you can get its positive effects, just like a snowball. Confidence is a simple tool to increase your mental power. There is a cycle that will help you learn how the confidence works:

Negative Cycle of Confidence

Positive Cycle of Confidence

Simple Steps to Gain Confidence with NLP

There are some simple steps that can help you to increase your self-esteem and brain power at the same time:

Understand Confidence

If you have an awe, you are reminding yourself that fear is an influential thing. You should understand that the confidence is an emotional loop in the limbic system of your brain. It is important to have complete faith in your confidence.

Golden Aura

Just imagine that you are an extremely confident person and there is a golden aura surrounding you. Imagine that you are walking with a group of strangers and starts communication with them. They love your personality because of your confidence and friendly nature. Always take this aura with you and you will feel confident in the atmosphere.

100 Percent Confidence in a Familiar Setting

Imagine a setting in which you are enjoying and feeling safe, such as reading a book, talking to your friends and enjoying time at a beach with your friends. You should pay attention to a relaxed posture and describe yourself in its setting. It will help you to feel relaxed and do lots of knowledgeable things. This practice will keep you relaxed and increase your confidence.

100 Percent Confidence in Unknown Setting

Now imagine a setting in which you are talking to strangers with 100 percent confidence. You are walking in a park, enjoying in a party and the strangers are giving you a smile. You should feel that they are interested in you and your personality. Feel this confidence and practice this frequently to increase your confidence level.

Take Your Snapshot

After practicing these things, you should take a snapshot of your confidence in a strange world. Memorize yourself that you are capable of handling everything with confidence. This memory will help you to build self-confidence because your unconscious mind is not able to understand the difference between imaginations and reality. It will be good to practice this several times.

Get Advantage of Anchor

Stick to your imaginations and flooded your mind with confident imaginations. You should go to step one and repeat everything. You will be able to understand that confidence is a tiny loop in the mind and you can switch to it:

- Feel confident to appear confident

- Appear confident to get positive reactions from people

- Positive reactions of people will reinforce your confidence

- Go back to the first phase

Gain Confidence with a Falsify Exercise

- Stand in an open posture without folding legs and arms

- Keep your shoulders relaxed and stand your neck tall

- Speak clearly with a good volume

- Don't judge others and focus on yourself only

- Directly talk to your subconscious and teach useful things

Practice this exercise frequently and enjoy its positive results in your life.

Chapter 3 – Get Rid of Fears and Phobias to build Self-Confidence

Usually, people assume so many things on a regular basis, but the response of different events may vary based on particular circumstances. Your subconscious usually focuses on the highly emotional thoughts to decide what is important for you. The subconscious is often bombarded with millions of thoughts and information from the temperature of the surroundings to the different body functions and noises in the background. The brain is as a storehouse of lots of thoughts, and there should be a better way for the brain to filter important details. Your brain notices the emotional intensity associated with any thought. The brain sort out information associated with highest emotions and the other things are thrown back in the unsorted precipitous heap.

For instance, your marriage is an emotional day, and your brain will not forget this incident. If your beloved person dies, you will experience highly intense emotions with this news and your brain also sorts it out as an important piece of information. Your decisions are often based on the detailed cataloging of the current events. Take a moment and consider the pattern of your thoughts, and you will come to know that your thoughts are directly associated with your decision-making ability. Negative thoughts can suck up your motivation because these natural vampires can narrow down your viewpoint. It will block the positive side of a picture, and you will not be able identified the opportunities in hand. Negativity and negative thoughts can kill your motivation, dream, vision, and trash all your life goals.

Exercises to Develop Positive Attitude

A positive attitude is important for your success in life because it will develop confidence and self-esteem. The positive attitude will improve your overall mood because you can enrich your life to reduce the effects of negative thinking on your life. Following are some useful exercises that will help you to develop positive attitude:

Open your Mind

If you want to develop a positive attitude, you should open your mind to think positively and listen to the viewpoints of other people. Understand their viewpoint, and respect their thoughts and accept their suggestions and criticism with an open mind. Pay attention to their ideas and thoughts to find endless opportunities for you.

Write Down 10 Things you are Grateful for Regularly

You have to write down 10 things on a regular basis that you are grateful on a regular basis. It will help you to think positively, and you can easily develop an optimistic look. The practice will help you to be thankful for the good things you already have in your life. There is no need to write only big things because the little things are sufficient to see a change in your life.

Learn to Meditate on a Regular Basis

Meditation will help you to stay away from negativity, and you will feel physically better. The meditation is equally effective even for a person who is not spiritual. You need to find a quiet and peaceful spot to meditate. You can meditate in a quiet room to avoid any distraction. Focus on positive things while using different meditation techniques.

Affirmations to Develop Self-Esteem

If you want to develop self-esteem with affirmation, then focus on your strengths and the things that you can do well. There is no need to focus on your faults because it will hold you back. Don't worry about failures because the failures will make you strong. It will help you to look at you in a better way. Following are some positive affirmations to develop self-esteem:

- My self-esteem is escalating on a regular basis

- I accept my defeat and focus on its positive aspects

- I have trust in my abilities

- I am able to do anything

- My confidence and self-esteem are really high

- I can achieve everything as per my wish

- I love and trust myself

- I understand my abilities

- I can speak to the positive thoughts of myself

- I am beautiful and creative

Identify Negative Thoughts and Fears to Kill Them

In the first step, you have to ask yourself, either you have negative thoughts or positive thoughts for the major part of the day. For this purpose, you are in need to identify negative thoughts. The negative thoughts start with:

- "Can't do" instead of "can"

- No, instead of Yes

- Not confident instead of confident

- Failure instead of success

If you are feeding these thoughts in your mind, unfortunately, you are feeding the negativity to it. The biggest problem of this era is captivation of the people by their thoughts. You often let your thoughts control you, instead of controlling them for your benefits. It is important for you to learn control of your thoughts.

Chapter 4 – Tips to Understand Others with the help of Body Language

It is a common concept that your communication includes 55% of the body language because nonverbal cues are also important in the communication. The nonverbal cues are specifically important to:

- Detect lies

- Going for a job interview

- Going for a date with your love

Understanding the body language cues and signals enable you to interpret the message of others and form a strong bond after feeling the sincerity and honesty of the other person. The body language is extremely useful while talking to strangers because you can detect either the person is telling a lie.

Basics of the Body Language

While reading the body language, you have to determine the comfort level of the person in the current situation. You can discriminate positive and negative body languages based on the movements of the person.

Positive Body Language

- Moving or propensity closer to you

- Relaxed posture without crossing limbs

- Constant and longer eye contact

- Looking at the floor due to shyness

- Genuine and true smile

Negative Body Language

- Moving away from you

- Crossing arms and legs while talking to you

- Looking away at the sides

- Feet are away from you and toward the exit door

- Rubbing nose, eyes and back of the neck

A single nod will tell you a lot about the person and there are lots of body movements that enable you to understand the intentions of a person. The body language of the person may suggest you the nature of the relationship with the person. You should pay attention to the multiple behaviors of the person to get an accurate idea about his/her comfort level. Here is a comprehensive explanation to explain how these cues work together to uncover the specific situation.

Spot a Liar

The body language of a person helps you to evaluate the truth in his/her communication. It may not be 100 percent accurate, but it will help you to have a good idea about the lies of the person. A liar always seems uncomfortable while telling a lie because of the fear that the truth can come out anytime. You may be able to catch white lies, exaggerated situations and deceptions. Pick up some common cues to have a healthy suspicion of the person. The uncomfortable behavior of a person enables you to find out if a person is telling a lie.

Fake Smile

It is really hard to give a fake genuine smile because it comes from your heart and reflects your inner happiness. A genuine smile can be seen in your eyes, and it is completely difficult to fake a smile. A smile reflects your genuine happy emotions. An uncomfortable smile can be easily detected, and it will be a helpful indicator to find out either a person is telling a lie. A person telling a lie can make a fake story, but can't give you a fake smile.

Stiffness in Upper Body and Excessive Eye Contact

The liars try to be over smart while compensating their lies by trying to maintain eye contact and stiffness in their upper body. Excessive eye contact can give a signal that there is something wrong. Typically, people move while talking and don't make an eye contact for the extended period of time. You can feel the tension in the neck and shoulders of the liars. They try to make an unusual amount of eye contact while talking to you. People often rub their neck or eyes while talking, and may look away or other sides.

Context Behaviors

Pay attention to the context because the liars try to give more details of their fake stories. If you ask any question, they will take some time while thinking about the answer. This kind of behavior is linked with the negative body language and by noticing different things; you may get the right mixture of the doubtful behavior. You can learn about their dishonest behavior because the people may exhibit an awkward behavior on a constant basis. You can recall the facts and information of the person to detect lies. Facts and fiction can be identified easily; therefore, pay attention to the small details.

Evaluate People on a Date

Body language is a practical tool because the nonverbal cues enable you to find out the personality of a person on a date. It will help you to make a date successful because their facial expressions and uncomfortable feelings are enough to tell that you have selected a wrong topic. Pay close attention to the behavior of the speaker and listen to him carefully. His/her voice tone will tell you about the situation.

Initially, people may not be open while talking to you, such as they cross their arms, legs and keep a distance from you while talking. It means they are feeling hesitant. Your goal is to change their uncomfortable feeling and increase their comfort level. Let them talk openly by giving them welcoming gesture. Naturally connect them to encourage good body language, and offer a genuine smile to avoid distance at the date.

Effective Communication During Job Interview

The job interview is quite similar to the first date because you have to convince the interviewer to give a positive decision. The interviewer may try to create an uncomfortable environment to analyze your skills, but you should be able to handle stress. Any negative body language will give a wrong impression to the interviewer; therefore, try to give positive gestures. There is no need to overdo nonverbal communication because it will give an artificial feel to your personality.

The first impression has great importance because it will help others to take the right decision. You can impress others with your charismatic personality and demonstrate others that you are the perfect fit for this position. Discuss your positive body language to increase the comfort level of another person. Positive body language can increase your confidence because you will surely feel good about you. It will be a valuable tool because there are a few tricks to practice positive body language. Make an eye contact with the person talking to you and indicate others that you are paying attention to their conversation.

A little nervousness is acceptable because the interviewer will understand that a reasonable person may expect anybody to walk in a little bit tensed mode. It is natural because the person without any tension may feel overconfident.

Body Language is a Partial Picture

Body language is considered a useful way to communicate your message and understand others. It will be fun to understand the feelings of others in different situations. It is not a supernatural thing because you can only understand the nonverbal cues instead of reading their minds. The techniques are based on the clues, and there is no magic involved in this technique. You may play a close attention on the intuition of the human beings.

Facial Expressions

There is some basic facial expression to show emotions and these are recognized all around the world. Some expressions are genetically inherited while others may be learned or developed due to social conditions. There can be some minor variations based on the culture and region of the people. Some basic facial expressions are:

- Happiness

- Fear

- Anger

- Sadness

- Repugnance

- Surprise

Having a smile on your face means you are feeling happy, opening your mouth to shout and closing your lips tightly means you are trying to control your anger. Open mouth, wrinkles on the forehead, stretched lips, tensed drawn and upward and stretched iris means a person is having a fear of something. Raising your eyebrows and widening will give an indication that you are feeling surprised on a situation.

Chapter 5 – Identify your inner talent to do something creative

Human perception is really complex and it is quite difficult to understand the complex thoughts. Everyone has some creative skills, but they are blind folded about them. It is really hard to identify your brightest talents because you are often unaware of your hidden aptitude. It is important to explore your talent because it has numerous benefits for your own life. If you want to discover your hidden flair, then you may think out of the box and open your mind to increase the diversity of your mind and thoughts. The talent may come in any shape or size; therefore, you have to extend your thoughts to various areas of life. Keep it in mind that talent can be different from just singing, dancing or any other thing. You have to read your emotions to find out the accurate talent in you that will be really useful for your career too.

Look at Your Past

If you are trying to search talent for you, then start with your past and look at the things that you have done. Try to find out those things that you enjoy the most and feel excited. Ask yourself about anything that you always feel proud to do. It will be good to think about your childhood because your childhood activities often help you to find out your talent and passion. Your hobbies are really important because your personality is often based on your hobbies. To understand your hidden talent, it will be better to focus on your hobbies.

Think about the challenging times of your life and try to remember the ways that you have had used to deal with the tough situation. The challenges and difficult situations in your life are often proved helpful to expose your hidden skills. For instance, in a disastrous situation, you were really calm and helped others in leaving the risky place. It reflects your calm and alert nature and it is no doubt a useful talent.

Think About Things You Enjoy the Most

There are different things that can make you happy, and your happy moments can also helpful to reveal your talent. Find out subjects that you love to handle and focus on your behavior in happy moments. Focus on the comments of other people because sometimes the other people can dig out hidden skills and talent in you.

Evaluate Your Skills

It is really different between enjoying a thing and doing well. You have to understand the difference between them to find out a talent in you. You can't think that the things you enjoy a lot are your talent. Your hidden talent may be something that you don't like or even don't consider it in your life. It is important to think deeply to find out your good skills and talent. There will be some natural skills in you and there could be various tasks that you can do without any struggle. Don't believe others because you have to find out a correct person in you. Only you can tell about yourself, your behavior, habits and lots of other things. It can be an unusual incident or a strange behavior that may help you to dig out your hidden talent.

Think About Successful Times

In order to find something creative in you, it will be important to look back at your life and think about your successful times. Find out those times when you really feel proud and inner happiness. It will be a signal of hidden talent in you. It can be a huge project on which you worked indecently or a task given by your boss for the success of your organization. Your management and organization skills can be great for you.

Narrate Your Life Story

If you want to find out your hidden talent, then write the story of your previous life. It will prove beneficial because you will not only find your hidden talents, but you can also see your career development. Start from your school days and mention your favorite subjects, marks, successful incidents and grades. Write about your achievements and thoughts for the future. After this exercise, you will be able to know your priorities. This practice will prove helpful to reveal the priorities of your life and you will be able to focus on the growth and cultivation of your talent and dreams.

Experience New Things in Your Life

To reduce boredom and monotony of your life, you should keep some room for new things in your life. Working while sitting regularly on the couch after office or spending your weekends at clubs will not help you. There are numerous activities that you don't try even once in your life and your talent can be hidden in one of them. You need some time for yourself to explore your inner feelings and consider your priorities. Evaluate your regular actives and find out things that you can cut to save some time. There should be some good amount of time for new experiences. Spend one whole day with you, read yourself and find out your favorite activities and the things you love to do or the things that you even can't imagine doing. You can plan some travel on weekends because it is the most powerful way to find yourself.

Accept Challenges

Your actual talent can be revealed in a challenging situation; therefore, come out of your comfort zone and try to do something challenging. Try to tackle problems instead of running away from them. Offer volunteer help of other people, such as volunteer gardening will help you to discover your love for plants and herbs. Working as an assistant scriptwriter will assist you to find out your hidden talent of a writer. You can write a song or a poem and publish it on online forums because the comments from the people of various cultures and countries will help you to dig out your writing talent. In short, you have to find out your strengths and remove weaknesses and internal fears.

Conclusion

NLP stands for Neuro-linguistic programming and this concept helps you to exploit your complete mental power. It pushes you to the edge of excellence and do things that were difficult to you earlier. The NLP was described by Richard Brandler and John Grinder in 1970. This Richard is a self-help writer and the Grinder is a linguistic expert. They worked on previous concepts laid by the experts of neurology and linguistics. They typically focus on the use of both sides of brains and unite the conscious and subconscious minds. Everyone has an active mind aka conscious that helps you to keep awake, but the unconscious and subconscious mind is dormant.